Little

T|
an

**Alan and Linda Parry**

paternoster
publishing

Hunt &
Thorpe

This is the farmer.

He is planting the seed.

Some seed falls on the path.

The birds soon eat it up.

Some seed falls among the rocks.

The plants grow quickly in the shallow soil.

But when the hot sun shines

they die, because they have no roots.

Some seed falls into thorns

that choke the little plants.

But some seed falls into good soil,

and grows up big and strong.

Jesus told this story.

He said that the seed was the Word of God.

Some people don't accept God's Word;

Then the Word is snatched away, like seed on the path.

Some people don't trust Jesus enough;

Then the Word shrivels up, like seed on the rock.

Some people put other things before God,

choking the Word, like the
seed in the thistles.

Some people truly follow Jesus;

They are the good soil, and grow up as God's people.

You can read about the farmer and the seed in Matthew 13:4-8, 18-23; Mark 4:3-8, 14-20; and Luke 8:5-8, 11-15.

Copyright © 1990 Hunt & Thorpe

First published by **Hunt & Thorpe** in the United Kingdom, 1990
ISBN 1-85608-045-5

The CIP catalogue record for this book is available from the British Library.

All rights reserved. Except for brief quotations in critical articles or reviews, no part of this book may be reproduced in any manner without prior written permission from the publishers. In the United Kingdom write to:
Hunt & Thorpe, Laurel House, Station Approach,
New Alresford, Hampshire SO24 9JH

Hunt & Thorpe is a name used under licence by Paternoster Publishing, P.O. Box 300, Kingstown Broadway, Carlisle CA3 0QS

Manufactured in Singapore.

Reprinted 1997